CAREER AS A
LEGAL SECRETARY

LEGAL SECRETARIES ARE THE NAMELESS heroes who work behind the scenes in the big law cases that grab headlines every day. Only in rare instances do they find fame and fortune. Perhaps the most famous exception is Erin Brockovich, the brash legal secretary who fought evil big business and won boatloads of cash for a small California town where residents were sickened by corporate pollution. Her real-life story was a box-office movie hit in 2000.

Of course, not every legal secretary will catch the popular imagination of the public like Erin Brockovich did, but all legal secretaries are vital links in the chain of the judicial and legal process. Those who have been in the field for a few years know the law – often as well as the highly paid attorneys who employ them.

Legal secretaries work under a variety of job titles. The fictional character Della Street, from the Perry Mason novel and television series, was identified by Mason as "my confidential secretary." Most legal secretaries have more mundane titles, such as legal assistant, administrative assistant, or law office manager. Regardless of the title, they can easily be called the right hand of the lawyers.

Legal secretaries are on the front line of a law office, representing the law office as the first person clients see or talk to. In addition to clients, they deal with a constant stream of attorneys, staff members, expert witnesses, and other involved parties. Behind the scenes, they perform a wide range of duties. They prepare and help process legal documents, such as appeals and motions.

They write briefs, conduct research, complete forms, and manage tons of files, both digital and in print. All of this is a big responsibility that takes confidence and the ability to juggle many tasks and roles at the same time.

Legal secretaries belong to one of the most employable groups in the world. One important reason is that the skills necessary to be a good legal secretary carry over to many other positions, professions, and businesses. Jobs for legal secretaries are plentiful at every level, from entry-level all the way up to the positions paying $50,000 and more.

Getting started in this career is strikingly easy. A high school diploma and some basic office skills can qualify you for an entry-level position. Particularly in small law firms, lawyers are willing to teach bright, ambitious people how to be legal secretaries. However, the job prospects are better for students with formal training beyond high school. Many career schools and community colleges offer legal secretary certificate or associate degree programs that only take a year or two to complete. Program graduates are prepared to hit the ground running with knowledge of legal topics, litigation procedures, court filings, legal research, records management, legal terminology, and law office administration.

Most legal secretaries work in private law firms. Many others are employed by in-house corporate legal departments, nonprofit organizations, and government agencies. These types of offices are found all over the world. Because legal secretaries are considered an essential part of every legal team, they can expect to find jobs in almost any location they want.

Being familiar with legal terminology, court filing rules, basic legal procedures, and law office protocol is important. In addition to knowledge and skills though, it takes certain personality traits to be successful (and happy) as a legal secretary. Excellent communications skills are vital. So are time management and organizational skills. Above all, legal secretaries must be extremely detail and deadline-oriented, since missing a filing deadline could result in a default judgment (automatically losing a case).

For those who can handle the pressure, the rewards are great. Working as a legal secretary is being part of a team of dynamic, interesting people, working together in a fast-paced environment. Every day brings new and interesting challenges. The legal field is an ever-shifting landscape that is exciting, intellectually stimulating, and never boring.

If you are a people person who is interested in the law, but not necessarily law school, this career is worth a look. Getting started is easy, little education is required, the average starting salary is $35,000 plus generous benefits, and the work is satisfying. Sound good? Read on to learn more about how to begin a career as a legal secretary.

WHAT YOU CAN DO NOW

SIGN UP FOR ANY SECRETARIAL skills workshops or classes your school offers. You should also take as many English and writing courses as you can. As a legal secretary you will do much more than simply copying legal documents – you will often be drafting them from scratch. That means your writing skills are extremely important. You will also need excellent verbal communications skills. You can hone those skills through communications classes such as public speaking and debate.

Becoming a legal secretary does not require nearly as much formal education as other careers in the legal field, but be sure you do get the training that is required. Talk with your guidance counselor about putting together a curriculum that satisfies entrance requirements for legal secretary associate degree and certification programs.

Beyond preparing for the legal secretary program entrance requirements, concentrate on getting as much secretarial experience as possible, and learn as much about the legal profession as you can. Begin by practicing basic secretarial skills in your own life. Take a look at your school papers and other files. Are they organized in a logical way? If not, explore new ways of thinking about organization. Numerous books are available on developing organizational skills. Find them in your school or local library.

Fast and accurate keyboarding skills are essential. Start practicing now on your own computer. You can take a class in school or buy an inexpensive basic training program. Your school library may also have typing training program CD's, or information on how to download them for free. You may think that your typing skills improve simply by typing a lot, but quality matters just as much as quantity. It's amazing what a little training can do to correct your habitual typing mistakes.

Research the legal secretary career on line. Check out NALS, the National Association of Legal Secretaries. Their website provides information about the history and current developments of the legal secretary field. They may even be able to connect you with legal secretaries in your area.

Talk with as many different legal secretaries as you can to learn more about this career. Ask what they like and dislike about their job, why they chose this career, and what school they went to. Different legal secretaries will have different experiences and opinions, so get information from as many as you can. If possible, shadow a legal secretary to see what a regular workday looks like.

HISTORY OF THE CAREER

THE HISTORY OF THE LEGAL secretary goes back thousands of years to the beginnings of the written word. The Sumerians of Mesopotamia in 2500 BC were one of the earliest peoples to keep records, on clay tablets using a stylus (a writing utensil made out of metal, reed, or bone). Scribes, the historical equivalent of the modern legal secretary, recorded business transactions, the decisions of government and ruling classes, and religious stories.

Over the centuries, the scribe (meaning "learned writer") became an important and well-respected figure in society. Scribes were found in all literate cultures, though different cultures had different uses for them. Generally, they wrote books or documents by hand to help cities keep track of their records. They also took dictation from authority figures to record judicial, historical, and business information.

Thanks to Egyptian scribes, we now know much about Ancient Egypt. The scribes there supervised the construction of monumental buildings, documented administrative and economic activities, and recorded the oral narratives of Egypt's lower classes. Egyptian scribes were so valued that they were considered part of the royal court and were not obligated to join the military, perform manual labor, or pay taxes.

In Ancient Israel, scribes were considered distinguished professionals who could exercise functions we would now associate with financiers, lawyers, judges, and government ministers. Some Jewish scribes copied the Torah and other books in the Old Testament on animal skins using specific rules for writing. These were the first writing guidelines ever used. For example, they could only use black ink made from a special recipe, and each column of writing had to have between 48 and 60 lines. No letters could touch each other. The scribes had to wipe their pens and wash their entire bodies before writing the word "Jehovah."

The scribe reemerged as a profession in modern times in the form of medical and legal secretaries. However, much of its social, historical, religious, literary, judicial, and financial significance was lost in the process. While scribes had historically been mostly men, the new profession was occupied mostly by women. Legal secretaries were given clerical work such as taking dictation. In most professions, women in the 20th century were consistently paid less than men. Even by 1972, legal secretaries were paid $400 less per month than heavy equipment operators, even though the two jobs were evaluated as equal in complexity. The reason was that heavy equipment operators were usually men, and legal secretaries at that time were usually women.

Unlike the revered scribes of ancient times, early legal secretaries received little recognition. Academic literature discussing law firms and the legal field seldom mentions the presence of legal secretaries. The absence of legal secretaries in law literature reflects the stereotypical gender hierarchy of legal offices in which male attorneys were spotlighted as the brains and power of the operation, while female secretaries were considered unimportant and remained backstage.

In 1929, Eula Mae Jett set out to revolutionize the legal secretary profession. She established a group with several of her colleagues in Long Beach, California, to meet and discuss topics affecting their careers as legal secretaries. The focus of the meetings gradually shifted to continuing education for legal secretaries. The popularity of their group grew, and word of their success spread across the United States. The National Association of Legal Secretaries (NALS) was formed. In 1949, NALS began to hold meetings across the country that focused on the legal services industry.

By the 1950s, the legal services profession looked quite different. The duties of legal secretaries advanced, as did the conception of what women were capable of in the workplace. Men began working as legal secretaries as well. The level of training required for a legal secretary's job was rising, and job descriptions were constantly changing to include an increasing range of responsibilities. New job titles were created to represent every advance of the legal services profession. A person could be a legal secretary, or with additional training, advance into a position as legal assistant, office manager, legal administrator, or paralegal.

Towards the end of the 20th century, the lines between what legal secretaries could and could not do blurred as office automation provided more time for them to engage in work other than secretarial duties.

Advanced
legal secretaries are often expected to perform research or make administrative decisions that are unrelated to clerical functions. The amount and type of work expected of legal secretaries continue to change with the times.

WHERE YOU WILL WORK

LEGAL SECRETARIES WORK IN A variety of settings, including law firms, corporate legal departments, nonprofit organizations, and government agencies. These types of offices are found all over the world. Because legal secretaries are considered an essential part of a legal team, they can expect to find jobs in almost any place where there is a law office (or legal department) with a job opening.

Legal secretaries interact with a great variety of people. Because they do much of the initial face-to-face interaction with clients, their work environment is greatly affected by the type of clientele seeking legal assistance. Each type of legal organization caters to a different type of clientele. Clients for family law, criminal defense, or immigration law will generally have very different attitudes, which will be reflected in the corporate culture of the law office. Legal secretaries also interact with expert witnesses, opposing counsel, police, and social service professionals.

The work environment also varies depending on the type and size of a legal office, as well as the geographic location. An established law firm with high-profile clientele will likely have a more spacious and comfortable office suite. Nonprofit organizations generally have less money to spend on office space, so their offices may be more crowded and have less equipment and sophisticated furnishings. Some big city law firms employ dozens or even hundreds of people. The environment in these large firms is often fast-paced, busy, and stressful. Nevertheless, these are the firms many legal professionals strive to work for. That's because they offer impressive, sophisticated offices, more advancement opportunities, and more money.

No matter what type of legal office they work in, legal secretaries can expect to be set up with a standard desk, phone, computer, and filing equipment. Their job duties may take them beyond the desk, but in general legal secretaries sit for long periods of time answering the phone, greeting and speaking with clients, filling out forms, filing documents, and other clerical work.

Legal offices are usually run quietly so that the attorneys and other employees can work without distraction, and so that clients are not overwhelmed. Even if the office atmosphere seems low key, legal organizations are rarely peaceful or slow-moving. The legal work environment is exciting because there are always new cases being processed, new clients to work with, deadlines to meet, and new research being conducted.

The majority of legal secretaries are full-time employees who work a standard 40-hour week. However, if they are employed by an organization or law firm that requires administrative or research work outside normal business hours, legal secretaries may be expected to work a longer or more flexible schedule. If the firm is working on a particularly demanding case, legal secretaries may have to work overtime to keep up with the clerical, administrative, and research duties expected of them.

THE WORK YOU WILL DO

LEGAL SECRETARIES PERFORM THE daily clerical functions necessary to operate a law office efficiently. Their duties include standard secretarial work as well as clerical work specific to the legal profession. They are constantly communicating, organizing, and collecting information so that the attorneys who are their employers have everything they need to work efficiently.

As the reliance on technology has increased in law offices, the different roles of employees have also evolved. In particular, office automation and organizational restructuring have permitted legal secretaries to take on responsibilities once reserved for managerial and professional staff. Because legal secretaries don't have to do as much dictation and word processing as they used to, they now have time to support attorneys in different ways, such as doing research and drafting reports.

Legal secretaries use a variety of office equipment, including computers, fax machines, photocopiers, scanners, and video-conferencing systems. Legal secretaries are expected to be familiar with all of it. Sometimes they are even required to maintain and operate leased equipment.

Legal secretaries are adept with all the computer programs and Internet resources being used in their firm. They often complete tasks started or previously handled by managers or attorneys, so they need to know how to access and track any documents they work on.

A career as a legal secretary involves a number of different duties, which vary depending on the type of law firm, the employer, and the other staff members. However, much of the core work remains the same. In a typical day, legal secretaries may complete the following duties:

Receive and place telephone calls to clients, opposing counsel, experts, court officials, and vendors.

Keep intricate docket systems to track legal filing deadlines. Attorneys don't want to waste time wondering when things are due, and it is imperative that no deadline is ever missed. They rely on legal secretaries to keep them on track and on time.

Schedule depositions, hearings, closings, meetings, and appointments with clients. Attorneys rarely arrange their own schedules or track down contact details. Legal secretaries save attorneys time by doing the scheduling work for them.

Mail, fax, or arrange for delivery of legal correspondence to court officials, clients, and witnesses. Attorneys want to know that their correspondence is being safely and efficiently delivered, without having to arrange for it themselves.

Organize documents, case files, and law libraries. Law firms use an enormous amount of paperwork, both soft copy (digital) and hard copy (printed). If those papers and files become disorganized, the firm cannot run efficiently, and important information may be lost. Similarly, attorneys and their assistants rely heavily on law libraries to look up case histories and research. This is impossible if books are disorganized or worse – missing altogether. Legal secretaries are expected to keep all books, files, and paperwork of the firm in order so that all employees can easily find what they are looking for.

Draft and type office memos. Legal secretaries enable communications between the different levels of the staff. They keep everyone at the firm updated on important information and upcoming events.

Photocopy important documents and correspondence. Legal secretaries are expected to keep all documents on file and secure, which often means having several copies in different places at once.

More experienced legal secretaries engage in work that requires more in-depth legal knowledge. These individuals might do any of the following:

Review legal publications and search databases to research laws and court decisions relevant to pending cases. For example, an attorney might ask a legal secretary to verify quotes and citations in legal briefs.

Submit articles and information obtained during research to attorneys for review and approval for use. Because attorneys are held accountable for any background information or evidence they use in legal proceedings, it is important they know what their legal secretaries come up with is accurate and defendable.

Assist attorneys in collecting information such as employment, medical, and other records. Attorneys often do not have time to sift through files or stay on hold while someone at another office looks for the records they need. One of the main reasons they hire legal secretaries is to do this kind of leg work.

Attend legal meetings, (such as client interviews, hearings, or depositions), and take notes on relevant information. Attorneys will look to their legal secretaries when they need details from previous meetings.

Follow up with pending court cases by keeping track of the latest court proceedings and new laws that may affect the case. There is an enormous amount of information to process in the legal world. Legal secretaries help keep attorneys updated with details and current events that might otherwise slip by unnoticed.

Complete various forms, such as accident reports, trial and courtroom requests, and applications for clients. Many clients use lawyers because they do not understand how or do not have the time to fill out legal forms. Legal secretaries help save time and money by dealing with the basic paperwork.

Type legal documents such as briefs, subpoenas, discovery documents, motions, and pleadings. Experienced legal secretaries are familiar with the templates for certain documents and can use their legal knowledge to write the drafts.

Entertain or host people in public places such as conference centers or restaurants. Sometimes nonprofit legal organizations do fundraising through private or public events that legal secretaries are expected to help organize and host. Law firms may also host clients, associates, or donors at such events.

Manage the spending of money on each account they are overseeing. If law firms need to purchase equipment or fund a special event, legal secretaries may be put in charge of purchases and managing of funds.

Teach inexperienced attorneys how to create and submit court documents. Some legal secretaries are so experienced with the writing and submission process of legal documents that they can guide entry-level attorneys who may have extensive legal knowledge, but are unfamiliar with the basics of court documents and procedures.

The field of law has become too complex for anyone to know it all, so few lawyers are generalists. Law firms typically specialize in a particular area of law, such as family law, personal injury, criminal defense, or intellectual property. The larger the firm, the more likely it is to have more than one specialty area. In most firms, there is at least one attorney with expertise in each specialty. Legal secretaries must also be familiar with the type of law being practiced by the attorney they work for. This includes a working knowledge of all related forms, documents, databases, and legal publications.

No matter how much legal secretaries know about a given case or branch of law, they are not allowed to give out legal advice to a client. Only an attorney may do that. The main reason for this is that the firm may be held accountable if the secretary makes a mistake in giving out inaccurate advice.

Diplomatic Security Specialty

The Bureau of Diplomatic Security, more commonly known as Diplomatic Security, or DS, is the security and law enforcement arm of the United States Department of State. There are legal secretaries working for government agencies at all levels, from local to federal, and DS is perhaps the most prestigious. In matters of criminal investigation, DS is the lead agency in the US for cases of international terrorism involving US citizens. DS personnel conduct security investigations, issue security clearances, and conduct criminal investigations involving visa and passport fraud. Overseas, DS develops and implements security programs to safeguard all personnel who work in every US diplomatic mission around the world, and to protect classified information at these locations. Since DS is present at every US embassy in the world, legal secretaries working for DS are afforded an unprecedented opportunity to travel much of the year. They also earn much higher salaries than most legal secretaries. DS typically hires legal secretaries on the basis of their previous work experience and advancement. This is one case where education counts – usually a bachelor's degree is required to qualify.

The Law Firm Hierarchy

Some law firms (especially big ones) differentiate between different levels of legal secretaries. These levels depend largely on how long the legal secretary has been working at that firm, past work experience, and education. With each level, the salary increases as the legal secretary advances higher.

Entry-level legal secretaries generally perform secretarial duties while gaining knowledge of the firm and the legal information needed to advance. They often work in the "pool," available to any attorney in the firm who needs them.

More experienced legal secretaries are usually assigned to support a particular attorney. They may make administrative decisions when the different choices are determined by set policies.

Advanced legal secretaries conduct independent research and prepare materials for administrative decisions and briefs. They may also coordinate the different administrative functions of the legal firm.

The most senior legal secretaries usually work for a director or senior partner of a legal firm rather than for an associate level attorney.

It is possible for legal secretaries to advance to the paralegal level, but only if they complete the education and certification required. Usually an associate degree in paralegal studies or a bachelor's degree with a certification in paralegal studies is needed. However, some employers do train paralegals on the job. This means that legal secretaries may be able to advance to paralegal status without going through the extra education and certification, if their employer is willing to take them on. Legal secretaries have the advantage of work experience and research in the legal field, so they may be more appealing candidates for paralegal studies and careers than entry-level paralegals who don't have as much legal experience.

LEGAL SECRETARIES TELL THEIR OWN STORIES

I Work for an Intellectual Property Firm

"When I began my career 15 years ago, my only skill was word processing. That was enough to get me in the door of a small town family law practice. The first year was very confusing because there was no way to really grasp the big picture of what was going on. My employers were patient and taught me step by step, until one day there was no more need for training wheels. Eventually, I got my certification as a legal secretary so that I could move to Los Angeles and get a better job.

Today, I work in a law firm with about 50 employees. Our job is to protect the intellectual property (IP) of our clients, most of whom are biotechnology and electrical engineering firms. We do a lot of litigation, prosecuting both domestic and foreign patent and trademark violations.

I work directly for one of the partners of the firm. My main duties include producing the paperwork to be filed with the US Patent and Trademark Office (PTO), and maintaining the dockets (calendar of the cases awaiting action in court). I also spend a lot of time with clients. It is my responsibility to keep clients apprised of the status of their cases. Sometimes I help them with their applications for patents.

The world of IP is very fast-paced. There are always deadlines and tons of paperwork that have to be just perfect. Last minute filings are almost routine, and I've gotten used to literally running to get an urgent fax or meet the court courier with forms for last minute filings. Every day I start out thinking it's going to be smooth going and everything will be caught up by the end of the day. Each day is different – the only thing I can be sure of is there will be a new set of issues or demands.

The best part of my job is it's never, ever boring. I thrive on challenge and I still love the work. Yes, some days are harder than others, but I have learned how to prioritize the workflow so that when something urgent comes up, whatever needs to be done will be done. It takes a certain type of personality to handle it though. You need to be detail-oriented and very, very organized – not just on the computer, but in your head. Of course, you also have to be someone who can handle stress.

I would advise anyone interested in this kind of work to look for an internship of some sort. Most of what I do can't be learned out of a text book, you can't expect to learn it overnight. If you make it through the first year, you are on your way to building a great career."

I Work in the Nation's Capital

"I work in a firm with 200 lawyers. It still amazes me that I started my career with no legal background and a lawyer was willing to invest the time to train me. I don't think I'm special either. Anyone who is ambitious and can keep an attorney on track can be successful in this field. I am proud of what I have learned and accomplished as a legal secretary. I have met famous people, worked on important cases, and learned more than I could from any law school.

One of the great things about becoming a legal secretary is the endless array of opportunities. Law firms come in every size from single practitioner to the big ones like mine. The range of settings doesn't stop with private firms either. There are many public sector jobs with courts and government agencies. Also, many corporations have their own legal divisions.

There are all kinds of specialties, such as finance, international trade, civil trial, entertainment, and criminal defense. Those are just a few. Whatever your personal interests might be, you can target your career goals to match.

All this means that there is always room for advancement because you can go from a small firm to a bigger one, or from one area of law into another.

What I like best about my career is the excitement. The environment is inherently nerve-racking and most people would get dizzy watching what really goes on in a law office like mine for even an hour, but I love it. There are deadlines every day, clients get freaked out, and everyone wants their work done yesterday. The office can turn into a pressure cooker at any moment. After 20 years of doing this, I don't even break a sweat. I know exactly what to do to relieve the pressure and make it look like everyone was in a tizzy for no reason. I get a great deal of satisfaction from that.

My advice to anyone thinking of becoming a legal secretary is to plan on getting certified as soon as possible. It will make your career go much faster and smoother. That doesn't mean you have to go to school before you start. If you see an ad that doesn't say legal experience or education is required, go ahead and check it out. There are still many lawyers who will hire someone with no legal background if they see that person is bright. In the interview, dazzle them with your communications skills and self-confidence. Once you're in, you can start taking seminars and courses on the side to learn the legal terminology, document formatting, and all the other stuff you'll need to know for the certification exam.

Another thing that can really help you starting out is a mentor. In a small firm, a mentor may not be necessary since the lawyer who hired you will train you. In a larger firm, lawyers are under the gun to make their billable hours. They tend to get impatient and just assume you will figure out what to do. There are so many things a legal secretary needs to know – having someone to call on for answers is invaluable. Probably the best way to find a mentor is through NALS, our association."

PERSONAL QUALIFICATIONS

TO BE SUCCESSFUL AS A LEGAL secretary you must be organized, detail-oriented, good at following directions, and very good at communicating. All of these skills are used on a daily basis, though some different abilities will sometimes be more important than others.

Much of your success will depend on your ability to perform basic administrative tasks. Not all of these will be taught in school. You should have a knack for keeping track of things (both on the computer and in your office), and enjoy paying attention to small details. If you are frustrated by the minutia of office work, this may not be the job for you.

Legal secretaries are expected to perform research work, especially if they intend to advance in their career. Do you have an inquisitive mind? Do you enjoy reading and learning new things? Do you relish the search for specific information in books, databases, and legal publications? If so, you are definitely suited for this part of the job.

You will have a much better time as a legal secretary if you are good at working with different types of people in all sorts of situations. Good legal secretaries are able to listen to their co-workers, employers, and clients with respect and attentiveness. They are also able to respond with constructive comments and criticism. After all, the legal services business is about giving advice, even if it's not strictly legal advice. But sometimes this can be difficult. Attorneys have high expectations of their secretaries and may become impatient if they are under a lot of pressure – something that comes with the territory. Clients also come to legal offices with high expectations, often under stressful circumstances. It is only natural that they may take their frustration out on the first person they see. You, the legal secretary, are usually that person. It takes confidence to maintain a sense of calm and control. You can't be easily intimidated by demanding clients. You must feel comfortable communicating with people in positive as well as negative situations.

On the other hand, legal secretaries must be good at taking directions and deferring to authority figures. You will never be allowed to give out legal advice yourself. When clients ask questions, you have to refer them to the attorney in charge, even when you know the answers. Constantly deferring to your employer can take some getting used to.

No matter how smart and capable they are, legal secretaries have to check their egos at the door. Attorneys often rely on their legal secretaries to conduct research for them. Some even expect their secretaries to write their legal briefs. Any work you do will be used by the legal team as though it was their own. To succeed as a legal secretary you must be a team player who is happy to contribute to other people's work. If you prefer to work independently and get credit for everything you do, this career may not suit you.

ATTRACTIVE FEATURES

THE LEGAL SECRETARY CAREER offers many attractive features, starting with the opportunity to work with a team of dynamic, smart, and interesting people. The clientele of legal offices are constantly changing, so you won't have a chance to get bored with one set of customers. The ever-shifting landscape of the legal field ensures that you always have new and exciting information to keep up with.

As a legal secretary you get to perform many different duties. The basis of the job is clerical work (filing, organizing, filling out forms, greeting clients, and scheduling), but that is just the beginning. Legal secretaries can spend much of their time conducting research, attending legal meetings, and keeping track of the latest legal news. These activities lend the job greater intellectual stimulation than a standard secretarial position.

It does not take years of expensive education to become a legal secretary. Some legal secretaries start with just a high school diploma, learning what they need to know on the job. Formal training is advised though, since it enhances job prospects and it only takes a year or two to complete.

Legal secretaries have many opportunities to advance in their careers. Over time, you will advance from entry-level clerical duties to research work, administrative decision- making, and preparation of briefs. With additional training, you can even become a paralegal. Each step forward brings added intellectual stimulation, increased stature, and better pay.

Legal secretaries enjoy excellent job prospects. Job growth is expected to be better than average for the coming decade. The more experienced you are, the better the outlook. Legal offices abound across the United States and the rest of the world. Every one of them needs at least one legal secretary to keep the office running smoothly. With so many law offices, there is a good chance of finding a job wherever you want to live. This is a stable field, too. Because advanced communications and interpersonal skills are basic requirements, legal secretaries don't have to worry about their jobs being automated out of existence.

Unlike attorneys, who may have to work beyond the regular 40-hour workweek, legal secretaries generally stick to an 8-to-5, Monday through Friday schedule. You can expect to work in one place, your comfortable office. However, just because you're staying in one place most of the time doesn't mean that your days are always the same. Every day will bring new challenges and unexpected rewards. For the people person who enjoys interacting with new groups of people all the time, the daily routine of legal secretary work can be engaging and fulfilling.

The money is good in this career, especially considering the minimum requirements for entry. The average annual salary for an entry-level legal secretary is a respectable $40,000. Earnings grow with time, too. Those who stay in the field for more than five years can earn more than $50,000, depending on the type of legal practice and geographic location. The benefits are good, too – you are almost always guaranteed a benefits package with health insurance, paid vacation, pension, and retirement plans. Some legal secretaries also earn bonuses on top of their base salary.

UNATTRACTIVE FEATURES

THERE ARE SEVERAL UNATTRACTIVE features to consider before you decide to pursue a career as a legal secretary. To start with, legal secretaries have to put up with accommodating the demands of a wide range of different people. Attorneys and other staff members depend on their legal secretaries to keep the office running. If something doesn't go the way they expect, you may be the first one blamed – even if you had nothing to do with it. The same thing is true for clients. You are usually the first person from the legal office they meet or communicate with. If they are unhappy about something, or are in a rush, you will have to deal with their frustration and impatience. This can be emotionally draining for anyone.

Even though you are expected to meet all those demands, your pay won't reflect your level of actual importance. You won't be paid as much as a paralegal, and your salary may be less than half of the attorneys you work for. Being capable of handling the demands will get you hired, but it may not feel very satisfying once you're in the office and performing some of the same tasks that someone else is being paid much more for.

Legal secretaries are not afforded much autonomy. Those with more work experience are allowed to conduct research and make some administrative decisions, but you don't do this independently. You can only make decisions based on strict guidelines that don't allow you much leeway. Any research you do will be looked over and corrected by attorneys before it is used. If you are the type of person who likes to have control over your own work, these limitations may feel demeaning.

If you are a physically active person, you may find it difficult to sit at a desk all day. Legal secretaries have few opportunities to move around, and if they do, it is almost always within the office suite.

The legal secretary profession has a long history of gender bias and discrimination, both in the hiring process and on the job. The ancient equivalent of the secretary was almost always male. The scribe had many interesting duties on top of clerical work, including a role in the literary development of ancient cultures. However, as soon as secretarial work condensed to clerical and dictation duties in the early 20th century, women were hired for the job, while men moved into higher positions.

Age discrimination also comes into play at legal offices. Older legal secretaries are often replaced with younger candidates who only require entry-level pay.

EDUCATION AND TRAINING

THE EDUCATION AND TRAINING requirements for a legal secretary vary. It is still possible for a smart individual to enter the field straight out of high school. In lieu of post-secondary training, these beginners start with good keyboarding skills and simply learn the rest on the job. However, the vast majority of legal secretaries today have completed legal secretary certificate or associate degree programs, either at career schools or community colleges.

Basic office skills are essential to becoming a successful legal secretary. Basic skills include word processing, keyboarding, accounting, filing, and record keeping. Excellent spelling, punctuation, and grammar are also required. Some people advance to the role of legal secretary by performing clerical duties at legal offices without a legal education, but with secretarial training.

Graduates of legal secretary training programs can expect better job prospects than candidates without any training. Post-secondary training is relatively short, especially considering the solid career opportunities that await graduates. Certificate programs typically take only one year to complete. Associate degree programs usually require two years of study.

Legal secretary programs teach students general legal office procedures and legal terminology. Students also learn to produce legal documents, such as discovery documents, motions, charges, subpoenas, deeds, legal memos, complaints, pleadings, and briefs. A typical program curriculum includes the following courses:

Business math

Legal research

Records management

Legal technology

Business law

Legal transcription

Legal writing

Business communications

Legal terminology

Law office administration

Upon completion of a legal secretary program, graduates are familiar with court filing rules, probate and estate planning, proper legal symbols and filing techniques, as well as legal fundamentals such as employment law and torts.

Advanced Certification and Accreditation

Legal secretaries can choose to take a legal training course offered by the National Association of Legal Secretaries (NALS). The course is designed for legal professionals who have little legal knowledge or experience, or whose knowledge and experience are limited to a specialized area of the law. The course also helps prepare legal secretaries for the examination to become certified as an accredited legal secretary (ALS). Legal secretary certification is voluntary, but highly recommended because many employers look for it. It may also help legal secretaries who plan on advancing their careers by later becoming paralegals.

To become an accredited legal secretary, a legal secretary must have completed a certificate or associate degree program, passed a NALS legal training course (or have at least one year of general office experience), and sit for the ALS examination. The ALS examination takes four hours to complete, and is divided into three parts. The first part tests written communications. The second tests knowledge of the law and office procedures. The final part tests understanding of ethics, human relations, and judgment. Those passing the exam receive a certificate that is valid for five years. This certification demonstrates to prospective employers that the candidate is prepared and committed to the demanding and ever-changing field of law.

Highly motivated legal secretaries with at least three years of work experience in the legal field may take an examination to become certified as a professional legal secretary (PLS). (A waiver of one year of the experience requirement may be granted to legal secretaries who have successfully completed the ALS exam or other certifications, or who hold post-secondary degrees.) The purpose of the PLS examination is to certify that a legal secretary has mastered office skills, possesses a working knowledge of procedural law, has a thorough knowledge of the law library, can prepare legal documents, and is able to make administrative decisions. The PLS exam takes a full day to complete and is divided into four parts. Part one covers written communications. Part two tests the candidate's knowledge of office procedures and technology. Part three tests understanding of ethics and judgment. The final part tests legal knowledge and skills.

Legal Secretaries International awards the certified legal secretary specialist (CLSS) title in specialized legal areas such as real estate, probate, civil trial, and business law. To be eligible, candidates must have five years work experience in the legal field. A three year waiver for this requirement may be granted to candidates who hold a four year degree or professional certification, and a two year waiver for candidates with a two year degree. Unlike the ALS and PLS, this examination tests the candidate's knowledge of a specific field of law. Certification is a badge of honor for legal secretaries who specialize, or want to specialize, in a particular field.

Legal Secretaries International also confers continuing education rewards to legal secretaries who have passed a certification exam, taught a legal education program or led a seminar, attended professional enhancement programs, or written an article for a law related publication. The certificate of accomplishment comes with recognition in the organization's quarterly publication.

EARNINGS

THE ANNUAL SALARY FOR LEGAL secretaries ranges from about $40,000 to $65,000. The median is around $50,000. However, salaries vary dramatically depending on a number of factors. Different types of law attract different types of clientele, which in turn affects the fees lawyers can charge and the salary they can afford to pay their legal secretaries. In general, nonprofit law organizations have less money to pay their employees than do big law firms catering to high-end clientele. Lawyers working in the private sector typically make much more than those practicing in the public sector, which in turn affects how much legal secretaries are paid.

Geographic location has an impact on salaries. Areas with a wealthier demographic naturally support law offices that can charge more and consequently pay their employees a higher salary. Law offices in poorer areas, especially nonprofit law organizations, bring in a much lower income because their clients cannot afford to pay high fees. Legal secretaries in big cities often earn more on average than do those working in rural areas. However, big cities generally have higher living costs that must be taken into account when evaluating earnings.

Salaries can also be affected by competition – the number of law offices in an area. If a law office is the only one in a community, it will be able to charge more than if there were competition with other firms.

As with most careers, legal secretaries with the most work experience earn the highest salaries. Entry level legal secretaries can expect to earn around $30,000 per year, depending on geographic location and the type of law firm. Salaries are slow to go up during the first four years on the job, but after five years they start making big jumps. A legal secretary who has worked for five to nine years can expect to make about $45,000 per year, and those with over 15 years of experience earn $55,000 on average.

Many legal secretaries earn bonuses at the end of the year, which adds an average of around four percent to the base salary. Anyone working as a legal secretary can expect a generous benefits package that includes health insurance, pension, paid vacation, and retirement plans.

Some employers will compensate for the costs of continuing education and career advancement programs, accreditations, and certifications. Legal secretaries who advance to become paralegals can expect to make between $60,000 and $90,000 per year, with an average annual salary of $75,000.

OPPORTUNITIES

THE DEMAND FOR LEGAL SERVICES fluctuates according to the economy and the changing needs of expanding, aging populations. However, it is difficult to imagine a world in which individuals, communities, and corporations do not depend on lawyers to sort out their issues. Legal offices exist all over the United States and the world, and they will continue to prosper as long as civilization exists.

The job outlook for legal secretaries is good – better than average, in fact. Moderate growth in the legal services industry is projected to lead to growth in employment of legal secretaries. Increased demand is expected for legal services in the areas of elder issues, environmental law, intellectual property, international law, and healthcare. As a result, in these areas, new legal offices will open and established firms will need to add more staff.

Overall, the legal services industry feels little difference between good or bad economic times. The number of job opportunities remains fairly constant. The only real difference is where the services are needed. For example, economic recessions usually cause a decrease in the demand for legal help with estate planning, contract negotiations, and real estate planning. There is a sharp increase in the need for legal assistance in the matters of bankruptcy, divorce, and foreclosure. Recessions also create an incentive for legal offices to hire lower paid employees, such as legal secretaries and paralegals, rather than the more highly paid attorneys. This is particularly true for corporate legal departments.

Further office automation and organizational restructuring will allow legal secretaries to be more productive in the future, which theoretically could lead to a decrease in hiring. However, the basic job tasks are very interactive, requiring advanced communications and interpersonal skills. A legal secretary cannot be replaced by a machine and the job will never be automated out of existence. Technology can only enhance productivity and increase the level of responsibilities a legal secretary takes on.

Advancement Opportunities

Advancing in this career means taking on more responsibilities. Generally, the more responsibilities legal secretaries have, the higher they advance in their legal office. Over time, a legal secretary can move on from clerical duties to research work, administrative decision- making, and preparation of briefs. Although the job title may remain the same, there is usually better pay.

Many legal secretaries prefer to advance their careers by becoming a paralegal. It is a particularly good option since they are almost certainly guaranteed excellent job prospects. Employment of paralegals is projected to increase at a much faster than average rate – 30 percent over the coming decade. Paralegals are also paid slightly more on average than the most experienced legal secretaries.

As experienced legal secretaries advance to higher positions, they leave behind clerical work that needs to be filled by new employees. Their advancement creates job opportunities for entry-level legal secretaries.

GETTING STARTED

NETWORKING IS THE ACCEPTED method of entering and advancing in the legal profession. Check out what internships or volunteer positions are available at local legal offices, even before you have finished your studies. Getting hands-on practice in the legal field before you apply for a job is a great way to boost your hiring potential. It's also the best way to build your network of contacts. You may also simply hear about a job opportunity from a teacher who has connections. Don't underestimate the value of networking with your peers though. You may all be in the same boat now – still in school, without even an entry level job – but sometime in the future one of your classmates may have the exact connection you need to land your next job. If you give off a good impression now, you may get a recommendation in the future.

Start connecting directly with legal offices even before graduation. Because legal secretaries are partly hired on the basis of their appearance and communications skills, it is a good idea to meet potential employers or fellow staff workers face to face. Do your homework. Basic research will tell you the kind of law they specialize in, significant cases they've handled, and the general philosophy of the practice. You should know these things before you arrive. In the interview, ask attorneys or other staff specific questions about their work and their interests. That will show them that you are a dedicated and inquisitive person who remembers details and is knowledgeable about the field. It also demonstrates you are serious about the job – something they will remember when making the hiring decision.

The National Association of Legal Secretaries (NALS) is a major player in the legal secretary world. Take advantage of what NALS has to offer. For example, if you are considering becoming certified as an accredited legal secretary, a NALS course will help prepare you for the examination. Although legal secretary certification is voluntary, many employers require it. Completing the course before graduation can give you the competitive advantage over legal secretaries who have to enroll in it while they are employed.

NALS is also an excellent networking resource. Almost everyone working in the legal secretarial field has had some dealings with NALS. Stay tuned for local or regional NALS meetings that you can attend to learn more about the profession and to connect with important people. These meetings can be a great way to keep updated with all the constantly changing news in the legal field that affects you and your career.

There are many other ways to track down job opportunities in the legal secretarial field. You can use employment agencies, both permanent placement and temporary, that specialize in legal secretary jobs. Most cities have local legal journals that include help wanted ads, or you can check the help wanted section of the local newspaper. You can find a job through any of the online job boards, but the ones dedicated to the legal service industry are best. If you look up local legal offices online though, you will find that they often post their job openings right there.

ASSOCIATIONS

■ **National Association of Legal Secretaries**
http://www.nals.org

■ **Legal Secretaries International**
http://www.legalsecretaries.org

■ **Legal Secretaries Incorporated**
http://www.lsi.org

■ **National Association of Legal Assistants**
http://www.nala.org

■ **National Association for Legal Professionals**
http://www.nalp.org

■ **American Bar Association**
http://www.abanet.org

PERIODICALS

■ **Legal Assistant Today**
http://www.legalassistanttoday.com

WEBSITES

■ **Penn Foster Career School**
http://www.pennfoster.edu

■ **Berks Technical Institute**
http://www.berks.edu

■ **Bradford School**
www.bradfordschoolcolumbus.edu

■ **Simply Law Jobs**
http://www.simplylawjobs.com

■ **LawCrossing**
http://www.lawcrossing.com

■ **LawJobs**
http://www.lawjobs.com

■ **Paralegal Gateway**
http://paralegalgateway.com

www.ingramcontent.com/pod-product-compliance
Lightning Source LLC
Chambersburg PA
CBHW072315200526
45168CB00014B/1595